Dear Neil, Jeannie + Cameron

thanking

Kindness

Andrew and George

9-11-2015

P.S come Visit

This Island: Tasmania

This Island

Photographs, text and design by Mike Calder, unless otherwise stated.

Published and distributed by
Mike Calder Photography
ph (03) 6227 8649
fax (03) 6227 9649
mike@mikecalder.com.au
www.mikecalder.com.au

1st edition 2006
Reprinted 2007
Revised 2008, 2010, 2013

Calder, Mike
This Island: Tasmania
ISBN 0 9775492 0 8
1. Tasmania - Description and Travel. 1. Title
919.46

Thank you Jane for your love and support.

Previous page: Water droplets splashed up from the creek below freeze on the foliage on Ben Lomond, North East Tasmania

Printed by Everbest.

This Island: Tasmania

About 10,000 years ago, the rising sea level swamped the land bridge connecting Tasmania to mainland Australia. Tasmania's raft of about 5,000 aborigines, flora and fauna were then isolated until the arrival of Europeans in 1804.

In this haven, animals such as the Tasmanian tiger, Tasmanian devil and eastern quoll flourished, safe from the predators which wiped out their mainland cousins. Generations of Tasmanian aborigines were hunters and gatherers, living in harmony with the environment. They relied on the sea for much of their food, but also moved around to harvest seasonal resources such as mutton birds and seals.

In 1803 the Lady Nelson sailed from Sydney under the command of 23 year-old Lieutenant John Bowen. The 49 soldiers, settlers and convicts established a British settlement, bringing the inevitable clash of cultures and decline of the aboriginal population.

Over a period of 50 years, Britain transported about 70,000 convicts to Van Diemen's Land, establishing penal colonies at sites such as Port Arthur, Sarah Island, Ross and Maria Island, where convicts laboured in harsh conditions. In 1852 transportation ended and the name of the colony was officially changed to Tasmania. From the graceful buildings and parks of its cities to the colonial villages, bridges and farmlands, the rich colonial heritage of the English is very evident in Tasmania today.

But much of Tasmania remains virtually untouched by humans. The Tasmanian Wilderness World Heritage Area covers about 20% of the land mass of Tasmania, the 17 national parks range from alpine areas to wild, windswept beaches. There are more than 2,000 km of walking tracks, thousands of lakes and tarns, peaks and crags, button grass plains, remote and accessible islands and impenetrable rainforest.

All in one small area. In this book I have attempted to convey some of the unique features of *This Island: Tasmania*. I hope you enjoy it.

Hobart

Australia's smallest and most southerly city, Hobart (population 190,000) is squeezed into a narrow band along the shore between Mt Wellington and the Derwent River. It was first settled in 1804, making it Australia's second oldest capital city.

Sullivan's Cove (pictured) is the home of a fishing fleet and punts which sell fresh seafood from their moorings. Ocean-racing yachts tie up here after the famous Sydney-Hobart race, hopefully in time for The Hobart Summer Festival, the Taste of Tasmania and New Year's Eve celebrations.

Beautiful historic sandstone buildings, some dating back to the 1830s, surround Sullivan's Cove. Many of these have been converted into art galleries, craft shops, theatres and restaurants. The warehouses that line nearby Salamanca Place were the centre of Hobart Town's trade and commerce in the colony's early days. On Saturdays they overlook the famous Salamanca Market which hosts over 300 stalls.

Historic Hobart

In February 1804 Lieutenant - Governor David Collins stepped ashore at Sullivans Cove and the settlement of Hobart Town began. By 1827 it was a thriving port with a population of 5,000 people. It was a centre of trade for sealers and whalers and Battery Point (above) was home to the merchants, mariners and labourers of Hobart Town. Here narrow laneways weave past grand mansions, tiny workmen's cottages and busy boatyards. The buildings are beautifully preserved and many are classified by the National Trust.

Described by Noel Coward as "a dream of a theatre", the magnificent Theatre Royal was constructed in 1837 and is Australia's oldest theatre. Saved from demolition several times, a fire damaged much of the theatre in 1984, but a fundraising appeal was lauched and it opened again in 1986.

Mt Wellington

When Hobart's residents return to the city they know they are back home when they see "The Mountain". Much-loved Mt Wellington (1271m provides a dramatic backdrop to Hobart and is criss-crossed by many walking trails, providing a wilderness experience close to the city. George Bass climbed the mountain in 1798, encountered an aborigine and walked with him for a while. In 1836 Charles Darwin also climbed it, commenting on the "noble forest". These days a short drive from the city takes you from rainforest right up to the windswept sub-alpine environment at the top, where you are rewarded with some wonderful views.

The Huon District

Hastings Caves' magnificent chambers began forming about 40 million years ago from dolomite rock. The Tahune Airwalk (bottom left) takes visitors at tree-top level to the junction of the Picton and Huon Rivers, 48 metres above river level. Franklin (below) and Port Cygnet (right) are small settlements on the Huon.

A river of many moods, the Huon River flows from Lake Pedder through the remote south-west wilderness to the orchards of the Huon District, where it becomes a broad, tranquil waterway.

Bruny Island

Bruny Island is off the south-eastern coast of Tasmania, separated from the mainland by the D'Entrecasteaux Channel. Both the island and the channel are named after French explorer Bruni d'Entrecasteaux, who discovered it to be an island in 1792. Its traditional Aboriginal name was Alonnah Lunawanna, which survives as the name of two island settlements, Alonnah and Lunawanna.

North Bruny and South Bruny are joined by a long, narrow sandy isthmus. It is classified by BirdLife International as an *Important Bird Area* because it supports many endangered species, including the Forty-spotted Pardalote, the Swift Parrot and 13 of Tasmania's 14 endemic bird species.

There is a growing number of tourism businesses on the island, including a cheese factory, oyster farm, vineyards and eco-cruises.

Richmond

The charming Georgian village of Richmond is one of Australia's most important historic villages. Many of its beautiful old sandstone buildings were built by convict labour and 45 are listed on the National Estate. They include Australia's oldest Catholic church, oldest postal building and oldest gaol. Straddling the Coal River and still in use, Australia's earliest stone arch bridge has been included on the National Heritage List because of its outstanding heritage value to the nation. Its completion in 1825 saw the town grow rapidly to be the third largest town in Van Diemen's Land.

Port Arthur

12,500 convicts served their time at Port Arthur between 1830 and 1877. They laboured in harsh conditions, isolated from the rest of Tasmania by the narrow Eaglehawk Neck. In the 1840s a system based on their separation and silence was implemented. During this time the penal colony was nearly self-sufficient, producing ships, sawn timber, clothing, boots, bricks and furniture. The church was built by convicts in 1836-7, but was never consecrated as all religions used it. By the 1840s it had a wooden spire, eight bells and could hold 1000 convicts as well as 200 officials. It was destroyed by fire in 1884. The Guard Tower (top right), built in 1836 with stones shaped by the teenage convicts at Point Puer, protected the military compound.

The Penitentiary building was reputedly the largest building in Australia when it was built in 1844. It was originally designed as a huge granary and flour mill, the mill being powered by a 24-man treadmill. A decade later the two lower storeys were converted into 136 single cells. Dormitories also housed 513 prisoners.

The Tasman Peninsula

The first European settlement of the Tasman Peninsula was at Port Arthur because it was easily accessible by sea, but separated from the rest of Tasmania by the narrow Eaglehawk Neck. In convict times the neck was manned by guards and dogs to stop prisoners escaping.

The Tasman Peninsula is well known for its coastline and high coastal cliffs, rising 300m above the sea at Cape Pillar. The Tessellated Pavement (far left) looks like it was laid by a bricklayer, and Crescent Bay (left) is just one of many picturesque beaches.

New Norfolk

Irish rebel Denis McCarty was one of the convicts on the Lady Nelson, which sailed into the Derwent to establish a British settlement in 1803. In 1808 he was the first police constable to be assigned to the Derwent Valley district in response to the large number of people from Norfolk Island who had settled in the area - hence the name New Norfolk. The construction of a road to the district combined with easy river access saw an influx of settlers. By the 1860s the Derwent Valley had become the primary hop growing area in Tasmania and oast houses were built to process the hops prior to sending them to the breweries. Today New Norfolk is a picturesque town of 5,000 people, boasting the oldest church in Australia (St Matthew's, consecrated in 1828) and the oldest continuously licensed hotel in Australia (the Bush Inn, established in 1815).

About an hour's drive from Hobart, Mt Field National Park is the second-oldest national park in Australia. Just near the park entrance, a short path leads past some huge swamp gums (Eucalyptus Regnans, the tallest hardwood trees in the world) to the delightful Russell Falls, which tumbles 40 metres over two tiers to the rainforest below. Higher up in the park is an area of sub-alpine wilderness and glacially-formed lakes. At Lake Dobson (far left), an ancient pencil pine greets the morning sun. These trees grow slowly and can live up to 1300 years.

The South West

The Tasmanian Wilderness World Heritage Area covers about 20% of the area of Tasmania. The South West National Park is the largest of the three parks in the WHA and features some of the most wild and remote coastlines in the world. Access to the southern part of the park is only by sea, light airplane to a remote airstrip at Melaleuca, or by walking the renowned South Coast Track and South West Cape Track.

Set 900 metres high in the Denison Range, Lake Rhona (far left) with its white sandy beach is one of Tasmania's many gems. Lake Rhona was formed when the Rhona Glacier carved a basin into the conglomerate rock of Reed's Peak.

The Franklin

In 1982 the Franklin - Gordon Wild Rivers National Park was declared a world heritage area. This is one of the three temperate wilderness areas left in the Southern Hemisphere and is home to many plants and animals not found anywhere else in the world.

The Franklin River is the only major river in Tasmania that's not been dammed. From the Cheyne Range at 1400m, it flows unhindered for 120km through one of the most rugged and inaccessible areas on Earth to join the Gordon River at almost sea level. A ten-day rafting trip is just about the only way to see the Franklin.

Right - a camping spot just below Newland Cascades. Far right - rafters enter Thunderush Rapid in the Great Ravine, rock-carved sculptures on the Lower Franklin (photos by Jenny Calder). Opposite left - the view from the top of the mast of Stormbreaker, on the Gordon River (photography and feet by Anthony Mann).

In 1980, the Tasmanian government unveiled plans to dam the Gordon River below its junction with the Franklin. In an emotion-charged campaign that divided Tasmanians, protesters mounted a blockade, during which time 1400 people were arrested and many jailed. The Franklin was saved by a Federal High Court decision in July 1983. This campaign was the genesis of the Wilderness Society and the Australian Greens.

The West Coast

Minerals and gold were discovered in the Queenstown area in the 1880s and the town grew rapidly when copper mining commenced in 1893. Trees growing on the surrounding hills were cut down to fuel smelters and when the topsoil was washed away by the area's heavy rainfall, the bare colourful rocks and lunar landscape we see today emerged.

The Abt Railway was built to transport the copper to the port at Strahan. Now reconstructed, the line crosses 40 bridges and traverses spectacular scenery. The Empire Hotel (opposite page), with its magnificent National Trust staircase (right) is an indication of the wealth of the region at the turn of the 20th Century.

Perched on Macquarie Harbour, Strahan served as the port for the Mt Lyell Copper Mine in Queenstown and was the base for bushmen felling the precious Huon Pine up the Gordon River and its tributaries. It remains a safe harbour for a small fishing fleet that braves the elements of the West Coast and is now the centre of tourism on the West Coast.

The West Coast

The Pieman is a major river on the West Coast

Mt Murchison reflected in the waters of Lake Rosebery.

King Island

Windswept King Island is 64 km long, 26 km wide and has a population of between 1500 and 2000. It stands guard over the western end of Bass Strait in the path of the Roaring Forties, about half way between Tasmania and Victoria. Over 50 ships have come to grief on the 145 km of coastline and Australia's worst maritime disaster occurred in 1845 when the Cataraqui, an immigrant ship from Liverpool, went down just 150 yards offshore, drowning 399 people. King Island is noted for its production of cheese, lobsters, kelp, and beef.

The North West

Windswept Cape Grim claims to have the purest air anywhere in the world, the nearest land mass on 40 degrees south being South America - 16,000km away. This makes it an important air monitoring station for the world, measuring green house gases as well as chemicals which deplete the ozone layer. The station has measured a 10% increase in carbon dioxide since it started operations in 1976. The Woolnorth Wind Farm harnesses the wind to generate power for Tasmania's grid. Each of the 37 towers is 60 m high, has a blade diameter of 66 m and operates most efficiently in wind speeds between 55 and 90 km per hour, making them ideally suited to conditions at Cape Grim.

Stanley

Dominating Circular Head is a prominent volcanic plug known as The Nut, 152 m high (opposite). Snuggled up against it are the original cottages and shops of the historic township of Stanley, established in 1826 by the Van Diemen's Land Company. The Stanley Hotel (below left) was built in the 1830s and is just one of the many beautifully preserved buildings in Stanley. Joseph Lyons was born in the humble cottage (left) in the shadow of The Nut in 1879 and spent his early childhood there. He was Premier of Tasmania from 1921 to 1928 and Prime Minister of Australia from 1932 until his death in office in 1939. Four years later his wife Dame Enid Lyons became the first woman in the House of Representatives and later the first woman member of Federal Cabinet. Joseph and Enid raised eleven children.

Devonport

Twin sister ships Spirit of Tasmania 1 and Spirit of Tasmania 2 criss-cross Bass Strait daily between Melbourne and Devonport. Bass Strait is only 240 km wide, but is only 50 metres deep on average and hence is one of the roughest stretches of water in the world.

The first view of Tasmania for passengers is the Mersey Bluff Lighthouse (1889), which guards the entrance to the Mersey River at Devonport.

Devonport is situated in the centre of Tasmania's north coast and with 25,000 people is Tasmania's third-largest city. The region around it is known as Australia's market garden. The chocolate-brown fertile soils produce onions, potatoes, peas, carrots and beans, which provide the bulk of Australia's frozen vegetables.

Cradle Mountain

Cradle Mountain was named by Joseph Fossey in 1827 because of its resemblance to a baby's cradle. Like many of the dolerite-capped mountains of Tasmania, its jagged profile was sculpted when glaciers gouged it in the last ice age about 10,000 years ago. On January 4 1910, Gustav Weindorfer drew breath on the 1545 metre summit of Cradle Mountain and proclaimed "This must be a national park for the people for all time. It is magnificent, and people must know about it and enjoy it." Cradle Mountain was set aside as a "scenic reserve and wildlife sanctuary" in 1922 and finally became a national park in 1971.

The Overland Track

Most people take 5-6 days to complete the 65 km Overland Track, the best-known of Tasmania's bushwalks. Starting at Cradle Mountain, walkers head south through stunning mountain scenery, lush rainforest and alpine vegetation before finishing at Lake St Clair. Near Pelion Hut in the centre of the park is Lake Ayr (right), nestled below Mt Oakleigh. Nearby, Douglas Creek (opposite page) flows through a moss-covered gorge just before entering Pelion Plains. At the southern end of the walk, the Mersey River plunges over Hartnett Falls, named after Paddy Hartnett who was an early pioneer who scraped a living as a guide and hunter in the area.

Lake St Clair

Over the last 2 million years, glaciers have gouged out Lake St Clair, headwaters of the Derwent River and Australia's deepest natural lake at 200m. Rainforest species such as myrtle and sassafras thrive around the lake's edges. The Echo Point hut is a favourite stop-over for bushwalkers.

The Wombat and the Devil

Tasmania's common wombat (Vombatus ursinus tasmaniensis) is one of our most endearing marsupials and is found throughout Tasmania, from coastal to alpine areas. Its short, strong legs are used to dig burrows up to 20 m long and more than 2 m below the ground, with numerous connecting tunnels and entrances. The female has a backward opening pouch to prevent dirt and debris entering while burrowing. The young remains in the pouch for about six months and stays with its mother until about 18 months old. Wombats are best seen at dusk when they come out to graze on native grasses and shrubs.

The Tasmanian Devil used to be widespread in Australia, but disappeared from the mainland before European settlement, possibly due to the spread of dingoes. Today it can be found only in Tasmania, anywhere from the coast to the mountains. Early settlers named it because of its fierce look, bad temper and wild screeches. The devil is nocturnal, sleeping in a den by day and emerging at night to feed. It is a carnivorous marsupial and usually scavenges for its meals, but it can hunt, its powerful jaws enabling it to completely devour all of its prey - meat, bones and fur. The young are born in April and the mother carries them in her backward-opening pouch for four months. By December the young are living independently.

The Midlands

The highway between Hobart and Launceston follows the old coach route carved out by convicts in the early 1800s, where relays of horses changing every ten miles could complete the journey in 15 hours. Along this route there are many beautifully preserved townships now by-passed by the highway. At Ross, one of the oldest and most beautiful bridges in Australia was built by convicts in 1836 (far right). The convict stonemason Daniel Herbert won a pardon for his 186 carvings on the bridge.

The Callington Mill (right) was built at Oatlands in 1837 and is the third oldest windmill in Australia and one of only four remaining.

Launceston

Settled by Europeans in 1806, Launceston (population 100,000) is Tasmania's second largest and Australia's third-oldest city. Situated where the North and South Esk Rivers join to form the Tamar River, it is an attractive city with beautiful parks and gardens. It has managed to retain much of its heritage and architecture and with the largest collection of 19th century buildings in the country, some of the best examples of Edwardian, Victorian and Federation architecture can be found. John Batman planned the city of Melbourne from his residence in Launceston and put together the syndicate to sail across Bass Strait to begin the township.

Cataract Gorge

Just fifteen minutes walk from Launceston's city centre, the South Esk cascades through Cataract Gorge. From historic Kings Bridge (below) which was floated into place in 1867, a path clinging to a cliff face leads to a beautiful Victorian garden with exotic trees, peacocks and a rotunda. From here you can choose to cross the gorge by a suspension bridge which was built in 1895, or the longest single-span chairlift in the world (308 metres).

The Tamar Valley

The Tamar River runs from Launceston through Tasmania's premier wine district, passing under the Batman Bridge on the way to its mouth at Low Head. Established in 1805 to help ships navigate the dangerous entrance to the Tamar, the Low Head Pilot Station (opposite) is the oldest pilot station in Australia to operate continuously from its original site.

Bridestowe Lavender Farm

The Bridestowe Estate was established in 1921 and is one of the world's largest commercial lavender farms, producing the fine quality lavender flowers and oil used traditionally in the perfumery industry. The 48 hectare farm is a spectacular sight in December and January when the lavender is in flower. In early January the five week harvesting operation packs the flowers into bins ready for distillation on site. 70% of the crop is distilled and the rest is sun-dried for the dried flower industry. It takes 10 tonnes of flowers to produce 1 tonne of dried flowers.

In the distillery, steam is passed through the flowers, causing the oil to vaporise. The vapour then flows to the condenser tubes, reverting to a liquid form where it enters the separator. After separation, the oil is stored in stainless steel drums where it continues to improve for years.

Flinders Island

Beautiful Flinders Island is the main island of the Furneaux group, a collection of 52 islands that stretch across Bass Strait between northeast Tasmania and mainland Australia. It's 62km long by 37km wide and about a third of the island is mountainous and rugged with ridges of granite running the length of the island. At 756m, Mt Strzelecki is the island's highest peak.

In 1830, an ill-fated scheme by the Tasmanian government to resettle 135 aborigines to Flinders Island resulted in the deaths of most people. Nevertheless the aboriginal culture survived and today over 16% of the population is aboriginal.

Most of the population of about 1000 is engaged in primary industry, with the main exports being cattle, lambs and fish.

The Bay of Fires

The Bay of Fires is a stunning region of white beaches, aqua blue water and orange lichen-covered granite rocks. It was declared to be the world's "hottest" travel destination for 2009 by international guide book Lonely Planet. Captain Tobias Furneaux named it in 1773 when he noticed many fires along the coast, leading him to believe that the country was densely populated. Abundant evidence of this occupation by Aboriginal people can be seen along the coast today. Middens indicate that their diet consisted of shellfish-like mussels and abalone, along with a small amount of seals and wallabies. The middens range in size from those that were used once through to ones that were obviously used repeatedly by generations of families.

Freycinet Peninsula

The beautiful Freycinet Peninsula consists of granite mountains surrounded by white sandy beaches, azure-blue water and orange lichen-covered rocks. The Hazards (opposite) form an imposing backdrop to Coles Bay and are spectacular at sunrise and sunset.

Wineglass Bay

A short walk up a well-formed track to the saddle between Mt Amos and Mt Mayson rewards you with this magnificent view of the perfect crescent of Wineglass Bay (main photo), ranked as one of the world's top ten beaches by US-based Outside magazine. A more difficult walk up Mt Amos provides a higher viewpoint.

Maria Island

The peace of Maria Island belies its turbulent past. For thousands of years the Tyreddeme Aboriginal people journeyed regularly to the island prior to it becoming a convict settlement in 1825. The island's 14 convict buildings and ruins have remained relatively unchanged since the convict era.

In the 1880s the Italian entrepreneur Diego Bernacchi set up island enterprises including silk and wine production and a cement factory, all of which subsequently failed.

The entire island is a now a national park, part of which is a marine area.